THE CHOICES JUSTICES MAKE